TEACHING OF HISTORY SERIES

Number 59



# HISTORICAL FICTION IN THE CLASSROOM

*Vivienne Little and Trevor John*



*Published by The Historical Association*

ACKNOWLEDGEMENTS

We are grateful to Dorothy Atkinson, David Evans, Beryl Jones, Beryl Morris, all the teachers and pupils who contributed and, most of all, to Professor Gordon Batho for his patience with the work's lengthy period of gestation.



ISBN 0 85278 281 0

Designed by Colin Barker

Originated and published by The Historical Association and printed in Great Britain by The Chameleon Press Limited, 5-25 Burr Road, Wandsworth, London SW18 4SG

# • *Contents* •

# • *Historical Fiction and Historical Understanding*

*Truth in her dress finds facts too tight: in fiction she moves with ease,* Tagore

There is a dark secret in the heart of many an historian and history teacher: it is that they first became hooked on history through reading historical novels. Perversely, at best out of more mature regard for the discipline of history, at worst to seem academically respectable, some later renegue upon those youthful delights and seek by evasion or disparagement to deny them to their pupils. Certainly they maintain that fiction should be kept out of the history classroom, where only such happenings and interpretations as are firmly grounded in historical evidence may be purveyed. Residual guilt leads even Professor Charlton, who concedes that 'concern for the ordinary folk of the past and insistence on historical accuracy' characterise children's historical fiction, none the less to assert that it 'obviously' has no place in class teaching (Charlton 1960, 1969).

We wish, on the contrary, to argue that historical fiction should be part of every child's classroom history diet, not only because it acts powerfully to generate curiosity about the past, but also paradoxically because it contributes to the creation in children's minds of a more faithful picture of it than that which they infer from standard school books or even from artefacts and documents alone. We submit that fiction helps develop the capacity for historical imagination which lies behind the sense of period and the sense of change through time and can also be used to foster the critical skills necessary for understanding the nature of history itself. In support of these contentions, we offer a number of case-studies by and for practising teachers who regularly include historical fiction in their work.

Since Geoffrey Trease wrote *Bows against the Barons* (1934) with the express intention of correcting the distorted picture of the Robin Hood period in children's stories and textbooks he has refined his techniques and employed them over a wide range of historical subject matter. His example has been followed by many others, history affording a rich seam to children's writers. Especially since the 1950s, a great quantity and variety of historical fiction, grounded in thorough historical scholarship, has been produced for children. Library shelves and children's corners in bookshops are full of works by Trease himself, Henry Treece, Ronald Welch, Cynthia Harnett, Rosemary Sutcliff, Frederick Grice, and, more recently, K.M. Peyton, Barbara Willard, Stephanie Plowman, Peter Dickenson, C. Walter Hodges, Patrick O'Brien, Robert Leeson and Marjorie Darke. They are given considerable critical attention by those concerned with children's literature. But no current handbook to history teaching contains appreciable discussion of their possible uses in history lessons. A Ministry of Education pamphlet (1952) advocated the use of children's stories in its suggestions for history teaching in primary schools, and E.M. Lewis (1960) claimed the superiority of historical fiction over textbooks where narrative history is concerned, at least for younger secondary pupils. *The Handbook for History Teachers* edited by W.H. Burston and C.W. Green (1962), offered an abridged version of Professor Charlton's pamphlet, and a list of novels considered helpful, again largely with primary school children in mind. D.G. Watts (1972) quotes a few examples, along with narratives about real historical figures in a section relating history to child development. Lamont (1972), Steele (1976), Garvey and Krug (1977) and Gunning (1978) do not mention historical fiction and Dickinson and Lee (1978) make no direct reference to it, though their insistence on the importance of imaginative work in history gives hope of things to come. In addition to Helen Cam's pamphlet (1961) only four short articles consider the question, the last in a brief but penetrating paragraph.

Helen Cam in her discussion of nineteenth- and early twentieth-century historical novels, and what they can do for students of history, affords pointers to the learning potential of mid-twentieth-century historical fiction for children, which now supplements them. Historical novels are a reminder that behind the statistics, ideologies, trends and institutions of academic study, there were human beings. Attractive because they provide a romantic escape from daily routine, they can, as they are seen to conflict with formal historical experience, actually encourage the desire to know more about the reality and feed the critical appetite. She counters the charge that training in historical consciousness and its skills is more properly pursued in the reading of good history which is also good literature, with the observation that the historian is restricted to his recreation of an age by the limitations of evidence, the inevitability of generalisation and the need for balance and proportion in judgment. The novelist is not so bound, is not required to judge, or to judge fairly, and can allow constructive imagination greater play. In going further 'beyond the information given' than the historian may dare, the novelist actually contributes to historical understanding, by offering 'a stimulus to the imaginative and critical faculties and an education in human sympathies'.

Some of these points are echoed by John Bradbury (1972) who asserts the capacity of children's historical fiction to interest and involve pupils in the past, to help the development of a critical response, and even, perhaps, to encourage the reading of history after pupils leave school. He suggests that historical novels are particularly well-suited to work in history with children aged 8-12 years and with slow learners of 13+. Anna Davin (1976) rehearses the virtues of recent historical novels for children in terms of historical accuracy and psychological validity, as against those older ones which nevertheless enlivened her own appreciation of history. She maintains that they can provide an aid to memory of past events, names, relationships, material background, beliefs and opinions. They offer a framework for the placing of historical information, and promote a sense of the continuities and differences between one age and another. Moreover through personalisation, they evoke an imaginative response without which history remains a tedious offering of half-assimilated facts and notions.

Tony Edwards (1972) contradicts Professor Charlton and states more emphatically than John Bradbury that good historical novels have a place in the history classroom. He says that although the history teacher has a duty to 'the march of events from Ur to Rome' and to world history, he is also increasingly urged to sacrifice breadth for depth. He knows that what is not enjoyed and what makes no sense in terms of children's experience or imagination will not be learned in any but rote ways. He hopes, therefore, 'to stir the imagination, heighten the awareness of the origins of everyday things, add another dimension to the child's view of his surroundings and develop some appreciation of very different ways of behaving and believing'. Thus the history teacher shares certain purposes with the writers of children's historical fiction, but if he is to tap the power of novels to evoke an active and inquiring involvement in the past, he cannot simply throw his classes the keys of the library. He must read the books with his pupils, discussing their portrayal of physical detail and the light they shed on great events, helping them to distinguish what is true from what is made up. For story tellers reinforce or complement his work. Ann Low-Beer (1974) claims that historical novels are undervalued as an introduction to history. She reiterates the importance of the imaginative route into history and the power of story to convey a quantity of information. Novels 'provide a bridge, an area where young pupils can begin to accept and consider all the many forms of the past, the ambiguity between fact and fiction, the relation of legend and story to "real" and, eventually, adult history'.

So there is some support in the literature of history teaching for the serious study of historical fiction in the classroom. What is clearly implied, however, is that if it is to have the more than incidental value which justifies its inclusion there, it must be good historical fiction. It is therefore necessary to pause and consider what might constitute good historical fiction in this context, and whether the history teacher, in seeking to serve his own turn, may do violence to the literary sensibilities a colleague is endeavouring to foster.

Perhaps writers themselves may provide some clues. First, they lay great stress upon research. Trease (1972) maintains that the historical novelist today has to meet standards of accuracy unequalled in earlier generations. Twentieth century historians have greatly increased the volume of information available about the past and the public is better educated. He saved himself from falling into one trap by discovering just in time a document indicating that heavy rain accompanied the swearing of the Tennis Court oath which he had set in beautiful June sunshine (1960) and was fairly caught by a young Scots boy who wrote in response to a Saxon novel to inform him that there were no rabbits in England before the Norman Conquest (1958). Hester Burton (1977) agrees:

*First, I must acquaint myself as thoroughly as I possibly can with the historical period and the events I am describing...I should be able to see clearly in my mind's eye the houses in which my characters live, the clothes they wear, and the carts, carriages and ships in which they travel. I should know what food they eat, what songs they sing, when they feel happy, and what are the sights and smells they are likely to meet when they walk down the street.*

So the teacher selecting a novel by a reputable writer of children's historical fiction today may be fairly certain that the historical information conveyed will be authentic. Indeed, Tony Edwards (1972) says of Cynthia Harnett that 'she writes better history than many historians, especially those who write for schools'.

Faithfulness to fact, however, is no guarantee of psychological veracity. Cam reports that Chesterton said of Henty's tales that 'the same very English and modern young gentleman from Rugby or Harrow turns up again and again as a young Greek, a young Carthaginian, a young Gaul, a young Visigoth, a young Scandinavian, a young Ancient Briton, and almost everything short of a negro'. Modern writers are acutely aware of the problem. Trease wonders how the novelist may create sympathetic characters who truly belong to their times and Hester Burton (1977) asks 'how can the most fertile imagination living today recreate the secret fears and unrecorded hopes of people living in past times?'. Historians of course have the same problem — 'the mind of the past is like a prism of which we see only reflacted light — light which has often issued out of hidden events' (Trevor-Roper, 1958) — and the solution lies in the same direction, that of total immersion in what is known of the period. 'I must understand,' continues Hester Burton, 'their religion, their political hopes, their trades and what is most important, the relationships between the different members of a family common to their particular generation.' What is more the novelist has a special problem here, owing to the fairly general supposition that children respond most readily to stories in which younger people, not too far from their own age, play a central role. Historians know relatively little about children of past ages. They are even more mute than humble folk. Ariès' work did not appear until the 1960s and even that is only intermittently enlightening. The demands of the story teller may be in conflict with those of the historian and the Henty trap prove hard to avoid. *Smith* (Garfield, 1962) is a gamin of many an age and clime. Much more is known about childhood in the nineteenth and twentieth centuries, but, by the same token, less will be taken for granted. Robert Westall did well to earn from a recent reader the following commendation — 'The language used by the kids was good because they talked like normal kids instead of talking all stuck up like in most books' (Atkinson and Evans, 1977).

This reference to literary devices leads to a further expressed concern of the children's historical novelist. He must wear his learning lightly. It must be integrated in character and action and not show obviously in explanatory passages. Despite his recognition of this, Trease himself sometimes comes dangerously near to the obviously didactic:

*'Have you forgotten the words our friend Erasmus wrote?' The Italian quoted them softly, his eyes glowing: 'The world is coming to its senses, as if waking out of a deep sleep. Still there are some who resist stubbornly, desperately clinging with hands and feet to their old ignorance'...*

and

*Italy has many such. They have a passionate love of beauty, above all the beauty of ancient art and literature...But they are also modern men, and modern Italy is a land of lies and plots...*

There are those who consider that Cynthia Harnett's work sometimes errs also, and Ronald Welch is perhaps the worst offender (e.g. see *Knight Crusader*, 1970, pp. 37-38). Trease recognises that many a book with unsound history is better literature than some in which details are impeccably researched, and, more subtly, that documented truth can *sound* false. (He was challenged for 'what the dickens?' in a sixteenth-century story, but knew that Shakespeare used it!) Moreover, Ronald Welch's fairly restrained description of the realities of Crusader warfare was attacked as too 'sickenly bloody' (1967) for the children for whom the book was intended. Nevertheless, Trease believes, and Margery Fisher (1961), a prominent critic of children's literature, supports his contention, that falsifying history to make a better story is a confession of artistic laziness and imaginative poverty. Some of the best work of modern children's historical novelists vindicates this thinking remarkably. What a lot one learns, for instance, from *The Namesake* and *The Marsh King* (Walter Hodges, 1964, 1967) about Alfred's times, or from *Simon* about the battles of the English Civil War, and yet the narrative power never flags.

Language is, of course, a problem. Faithful reproduction even of English until fairly modern times would be unintelligible or ludicrous, where it was possible, but Rosemary Sutcliff, while recognising that modern colloquial English may be the logical translation of medieval vernacular speech, still cannot reconcile herself to a Norman knight saying 'Shut-up Dickie; you're getting too big for your boots' (1973). Her answer is to try, in dialogue, to catch the rhythm of the contemporary tongue and very effectively she does it. 'Large ideas for yourself you have. Only the greatest warriors have their shield thralls behind them' (1959). Her narrative, witness *Beowulf: Dragon Slayer* (1961), like that of Jill Paton Walsh, is, where appropriate, redolent of much reading of sagas and powerfully evocative at least of the literary flavour of early times. Barbara Willard uses dialect forms to create a remote enclosed world. Other writers struggle more prosaically to avoid obvious anachronism, jarring slang and 'pishtushery'. Historians must convey a sense of period by other means than these, but novels for children whose language echoes contemporary literature can lay foundations for it, and the conscientious approach by their authors to the problems of dialogue at least helps to reduce the danger that imagined conversation may militate against it.

Another interest of these writers which may involve difficulties for history teachers is the choice and treatment of theme. As literary artists they are concerned with universals and they often claim to write because they have something to say about the modern world. In 1977 Geoffrey Trease said:

*But the second theme, the driving force to write...came from the television newsreel, showing night after night queues of prospective emigrants outside Australia House and similar offices. We were going through one of our wearisomely recurrent economic crises. It was 1957. The popular cry was 'England is finished'...I knew that the same cry had been heard in Wessex in 878. Guthrum seemed master of the last Christian corner of England. Alfred was 'missing, presumed dead'...'Deor's Lament' provided an apt text: 'That passed. This also may'. My other example is the highly topical theme of racial and religious toleration. I had long wanted to use an Andalusian setting and to depict for children the period when Arab culture had transformed southern Spain into a garden, later spoilt by the neglect of the Christian conquerors. The then tolerant attitude of the Arabs to the Jews, in striking contrast to the persecution practised by the Catholics, added a further dimension.*

And Hester Burton, again in 1977, said that:

*...as a novelist, I am primarily interested in one kind of story; it is the story of young people thrown into some terrible predicament of danger and scrambling out of it, unaided...For a novelist, such as myself, life is far too safe for the young in the twentieth century...history...is full of robust, exciting plots for novelists, who...wish to subject their characters to the test of danger...I am quite conscious that I choose an event or theme in history because it echoes something I have experienced in my own life. For example, when I described the autumn of Trafalgar in* Castors Away *I consciously relived the summer of 1940...In a quieter way, the themes of* Time of Trial *and* Thomas *echo a contemporary experience, namely the growing concern of many of us at the encroachment of the State upon the rights of the individual; while the theme of* No Beat of Drum *is perhaps the most insistently modern of all, since it is concerned with the bitter misery of the poor in a world of the rich.*

For historians the truth of events lies in their particulars. Modern parallels are incidential and may be misleading, as is the drawing of lessons from past facts. Nevertheless, it is difficult to deny that much historical work *is* inspired by modern preoccupations — the twentieth century is in some ways justly described as the century of the common man and it is surely no accident that twentieth-century historians, and not only those of the *Annales* school, spend so much of their time in search of him.

Good children's historical fiction, then, requires all the attributes of the good children's novel — the striking opening, the intriguing plot, the element of suspense, and characters who are interesting, who develop as the story unfolds and with some of whom the children can identify. Moreover it must take children back into an historical period whose way of life is unfamiliar, subtly supplying circumstantial detail of dress, buildings, goods, transport, tools, landscape and social organisation without clogging the tale with mini history lessons. It is, according to those who write it, fiction which exhibits 'the living changing elements linking the past to the present, without violating the essential character of the past' (Leeson, 1976) and creates through imaginative appeal a world into which children will willingly travel. These are among the aims of the history teacher. The similarity suggests that he might do well to encourage his pupils to read such books, and in order to do so the more effectively, actually to include consideration of some of them in his lessons.

Historical fiction helps children to make that imaginative leap into the past which genuine understanding of history demands. It carries conviction of reality in relation to the past. It does both these things by putting historical information into three dimensions. Compare two extracts from typical accounts in better quality textbooks:

*Most country people were villeins...Most villeins did farmwork for their landlord. For two or three days each week villeins had to work for their lord — ploughing and sowing in the spring, haymaking and harvesting in the summer. On the other days they were free to cultivate their own strips of land. Villeins were often very poor and found it hard to make a living* (Davies, 1972);

*Slowly William brought the country under control. He built a network of castles from which his Norman followers could ride out to stop any trouble in the surrounding countryside. Then he ordered a survey of England called the Domesday Book, which would show him exactly what his new realm contained, and what taxes its people could be expected to pay. It is said that not even a cow or pig escaped the notice of William's men* (Chancellor, 1967);

with one from a story of the same period:

*The following morning he and his father with five villeins set out for the shire-moot. They went on foot, carrying some food with them, as they did not expect to be home before nightfall. After walking for several miles, they reached the spot where the moot was held. A large crowd of Normans and English were standing behind a little group of soldiers. Under a tree, the Norman Commissioner was seated on a stool, and behind him the sheriff, a young clerk, and a man who looked a little like the bailiff of Halesowen. The clerk leant against the tree and wrote upon a piece of parchment stretched over a block of wood, dipping his quill into the inkhorn which hung from his belt. Gurth noticed Earl Roger talking to several other barons who lived in the hundred. He also saw the bailiffs and priests of the different demesnes, talking to their own villeins and evidently trying to explain points that were troubling them. There was a low murmur, but above it Gurth could hear the Norman's clear voice, asking questions, and the loud tones of the interpreter translating at his side. When each question was answered the clerk made notes upon his parchment. Gurth peered through the crowd when Earl Roger was called. He took the oath with a loud voice and answered shortly as though he were annoyed. His bailiff came after him, and then the priest and then the six villeins, all of whom took the same oath* (Power, 1953).

Historical fiction also achieves its purposes by personalising historical events. Compare the impact of:

*The Pankhursts soon found themselves the leaders of a great movement, whose members ranged from rich and elegant women to working girls who wore clogs and shawls. At one time or another most of the leaders of the demand for votes for women went to prison. This is because many of them thought that the only way to compel people to listen to them was to create public disturbances. In the early days of the movement they contented themselves with heckling at meetings and refusing to leave when ordered to do so. Even for this they were arrested and often treated roughly by the police* (Nash and Newth, 1967);

with that of

*'And in conclusion,' the magistrate said, looking disapprovingly over the top of his half-moon glasses, 'I would urge you to look carefully at your motives for such a disgraceful attack. You have behaved in an irresponsible and shameful fashion. The only mitigating circumstances would seem to be your green youth and the undoubted evil influence of the so-called leader of this...er...Suffragette movement you appear to have embraced. You are fined five pounds each, with seven days to pay.' Emily followed Louise as she limped from the dock, her heart filled with anger and despair. How would she ever find that much money in seven days? Five pounds...fifteen...fifty were equally impossible. Would she have to go to prison instead? People did; remember the time old Mr Nailor hit a policeman. She didn't dare look at Mam sitting pinched with shame at the back of the courtroom, or at Peter Marshall beside his frowning white-whiskered father — frosty devil! The old man had set up such a rumpus at the police station that night, treating her as if she was dirt, but she hadn't felt remorse, only burning shame at the failure. Mam was hurrying out now. Mr Marshall, grasping Louise by the elbow, was shepherding her away from the disgrace. 'I shall recompense the golf club, Louise, but your fine must come out of your allowance. And that is all there is to be said'* (Darke, 1975).

Here are a rich and elegant woman and a working girl of flesh and blood reacting to the response of the authorities to their work for their cause — surely more vivid and memorable and in some sense more true-to-life, though fictional, than the textbook account, and the first extract is taken from one of the better of its kind.

A further way in which historical fiction is an aid to historical imagination is what one might call the truth of setting. A history book for children may provide pictures and descriptions of the homes of people of differing status in the later fifteenth century, it may supply extracts from inventories and wills of the better off to indicate their contents, it may sketch clothing, list conveyances and the pace and hazards of travel, or refer to the importance of the printing press and the economic and social changes it wrought, but translating such information into recognition of the actuality of the past involves a greater effort of imagination than most children can manage. A story like *The Load of Unicorn* (Harnett, 1959), to take one of many possible examples, can help them to do this. A scrivener's son (and the story offers a vivid referent for that difficult word) cherishes his tiny attic room, minimal privacy and few possessions. He moves among the crowded and dirty streets between home and school. He encounters Caxton, a gentleman of higher status than his father, is excited by his first sight and study of a printing press, becomes apprenticed to Caxton and is involved in travelling to Warwickshire to secure for printing a manuscript of Malory's *Morte D'Arthur*. His own brothers — scriveners fearful of damage to their trade — have indulged in crime to prevent the printing of this manuscript. Thus a great deal of history can be absorbed effortlessly in the pursuit of a gripping adventure story.

But the benefits of putting history in the round are not confined to these. One of the more difficult concepts to grasp in history, particularly since it is learned bit by bit, one thing after another, is the simultaneity of events, and the fact that some are connected and some are not. Trease makes valuable use in *Trumpets in the West* of the fact that the first performance, at a girl's school in Chelsea, of the first English opera, Purcell's *Dido and Aeneaus,* occurred within a month or two of the Glorious Revolution, thus demonstrating that a period may be important for other than political reasons. Novels like those centring on the Crusades, for instance, which involve happenings in different countries, can help prepare that horizontal perspective which is so often a vital ingredient of historical understanding. Even more significantly, perhaps, novels can help the development of the concept of historical time. Characters grow up during a tale which refers to a series of well-known events, developments dismissed in a line in a textbook are shown to have involved several years of someone's life. Family sagas like the *Flambards* series reveal change and continuity over a considerable period.

Related to this are Rosemary Sutcliff's reflections (1967) upon the telescoping effects of the conventional periodisation of English history and the distorted picture it can produce. Wanting to write about the late Roman era, she paused to realise that the familiar dates meant that the Romans were in occupation of Britain for 450 years, that is as long a time as lies between us and the Tudors. Their withdrawal in the early fifth century after generations of inter-breeding cannot have been that simple, and the traditional picture of an easy Saxon victory over a people gone soft must be erroneous — after all the conquest took 250 years. Out of such musings grew *The Lantern Bearers*, and out of such imaginative stopping of the historical clock can grow much insight.

Important insights of another kind can stem from the change of angle afforded by fiction writers. Characters involved in great events like the French Revolution, for example, unlike the history textbook writer, do not know how the story ends, just as the people who made them did not. Moreover, events are viewed from the limited angle of single or groups of characters, who often see them differently, apprehend their significance, if at all, differently from the all-wise, all-knowing view almost inevitably characteristic of the textbook, if not of the best scholarly writing.

Historical fiction can help the history teacher by making clear the reality of the past, helping children to read between the lines of their history books and to know what they are saying when they say that some medieval people thought the world was flat, that before the nineteenth century it took a very long time to accomplish journeys which are now over in a few hours, or that it really mattered to individuals that the government introduced the Factory Acts.

A few extracts from reviews by children of historical novels illustrate the point:

- *I knew the story was about the past because nowadays to deliver mail they would use a truck or van and not a stagecoach. I learnt things we take for granted now were a lot harder then because roads had not been developed* (Adam Williamson, aged 11);
- *You knew the story was made in another time because everything was not expensive and their dress wasn't like ours today* (Elizabeth Gray, aged 11);
- *I could tell they lived long ago because of the names of the aircraft and the words they used like archie or flack for anti-aircraft guns* (Steven Keates, aged 10);
- *I could tell this book was set in a different time because it mentions rationing and also about the windows of the buses being covered in mesh netting to stop the glass being hurled at passengers* (Elizabeth Williams, aged 13);

and even confusion offers opportunities:

- *Another thing was that there was just poor family's [sic] but no gap and then rich family's [sic]* (Elizabeth Gray, aged 11);

and

- *I did learn that some indians [sic] had Mohican hair* (Gregory Manttan, aged 11).

History teachers discussing fiction read by and with their pupils can help the development of horizontal and vertical perspectives on the past and sharpen perception of the complexity of past circumstances and happenings.

There remains the problem of the fictional element. The characters and stories in the novels are largely made up and great men and great events are presented in ways that are at once simpler and fuller than the historian's knowledge justifies — simpler because novels can rarely accommodate the qualifications and uncertainties of historians; fuller because narrative requires details unimportant or unknown to historians. Does this not confuse children and contaminate their historical imagination? And, if personalisation is desirable, does that not merely imply that greater use should be made of historical biography and autobiography? There are some history teachers who will always feel that, and they can make a strong case. Moreover, it must be emphasised that there is no intention to suggest that children's historical experience should consist entirely of the reading of historical fiction. What such teachers ignore, however, is the age-old power of the story to teach as it entertains. Not for nothing are the myth, the parable and the fable universal devices of religious and moral education, and the same principle applies in other areas. Imaginative stimulus is a powerful aid to learning, as it is to memory, if recent studies of brain function are to be trusted, and make-believe is a natural activity among children, who are, however, capable of distinguishing it from real experience. Many authors point out the elements of fact and fiction in their stories for children to consider and if they do not, then teachers may. In-service courses at the University of Warwick have explored with teachers the possibilities of presenting, along with the reading of the novels, some of the evidence which authors used, e.g. extracts from *The Saga of Eric the Red* (edited by Magnusson and Palson, 1965) are compared with Henry Treece's *Vinland the Good* while Charles Hannam's autobiography *A Boy in your Situation* (1977) is put alongside *Friedrich* (1971) by H.P. Richter or *Fireweed* (1969) by Jill Paton Walsh. In distinguishing what is true from what is invented, children take early steps along the road to the critical appraisal of sources, explanations and interpretation characteristic of history. Biographies and autobiographies are useful, but how many exist at levels suitable for children and how widely do they range among the different classes of society, how far do they reach back into early times? There is plenty of historical fiction readily available. And how is the child to make the connections among the various biographies, which are made for him in story about a number of characters fictitious or real? Jesting Pilate asked, 'What is truth?'. History teachers who eschew historical fiction are guilty, by implication, of too hasty and simplistic an answer.

It cannot but be admitted, however, that force-feeding is no way to ensure the benefits of fiction. They will only be secured if children will read historical novels and enjoy them. There is some evidence from developmental psychology to suggest that they may, and that certain ingredients, such as adventure for the 8-12 age group and love interest for teenagers, are enticing, each of which many historical settings can provide. Norma Schlager (1978) for example, argues that books which reflect the unconscious preoccupations of middle-childhood with exploring the perimeters of reality will appeal to that age group, hence, perhaps, the popularity of books like those of Hester Burton and Laura Ingalls Wilder which emphasise survival. But Margery Fisher holds that it is the writer's business to provide a book which a child can use himself to confirm what he already knows or to discover something new. It is true that children like books of widely diverging artistic quality and they may prefer those which reflect their perception of the world, but it is reasonable also to suppose that wider questions of subject matter and style are involved and that choice is affected by what is available. It is not difficult to surmise from the large quantities produced that the type of children's historical fiction discussed here is sure to sell. Publishers' blurb direct much of it at the 8-13+ age group, and there is evidence that history is a minority interest from puberty to 16+. What we do not know with any certainty is by whom it is actually read. C.S. Lewis was 'almost inclined to set it up as a canon that a children's story which is enjoyed only by children is a bad children's book' and it is hard to meet a children's author who does not deny thinking of himself as such. To rely entirely upon developmental theory in selecting books, historical or otherwise, is to mistake description for prescription. Bruner emphasises the importance of agents in the handing on of the tools of learning. If a teacher is convinced that the type of historical fiction discussed here has something valuable to offer his pupils in their learning of history, he owes them at the very least an enthusiastic introduction to the genre.

Despite good sales records and critical acclaim (a number of authors mentioned above have received Carnegie medals for instance), few of these books are well known to students and teachers, or widely used in classrooms. The contention of this section is that the reading of historical fiction, both as a pastime, and skilfully led by teachers, is an imaginative approach to the past which can help develop historical understanding in children from quite a young age to well into the teens, because it helps to make concrete that which is essentially abstract. It presents the framework of characteristics of an age in a palatable and easily retainable form and aids conceptual development. Appealing to the imagination, it creates a positive response to the past, and encourages, in affording a model, the growth of historical imagination. Mary Warnock (1976) argues that children may be deprived if they are not encouraged to read and look at the imaginative works of others. History which displays the highest qualities of historical imagination is barely accessible to children. That exhibited in historical novels, which also draw upon and allow expression of these elements of fantasy and feeling so helpful to learning, can serve as a stepping stone to it, while at the same time vouchsafing literary experience at an appropriate level.

# • Historical Fiction in the Classroom

Teachers often argue that, while historical novels may well contribute to historical understanding, children do not *choose* to read them. Publishers claim to find them hard to sell (Wood, 1982). Recent researchers into childrens reading habits 'suspect that a crucial factor in the quantity of voluntary reading that children do is the time, energy and enthusiasm which teachers devote (or in some cases do not devote) to books' (Marriott and Kenny, 1984). Our experience in encouraging initial training students to introduce historical fiction into their lessons, and the work of practising teachers described below, testify to the validity of this claim.

## Case Study 1

*The Boy with the Bronze Axe,* Kathleen Fidler (Oliver and Boyd, 1986, and Puffin)

I was delighted to discover this well-constructed adventure story, describing life in a Stone Age village, which helped my class of 8-9 year old junior school children to understand living conditions during this early history period. It tells the story of Kali and Tenko and their friends in Skara Brae, Orkney Islands, as it may well have happened 3000 years ago.

Man constantly struggles with the elements and his determination is to survive. The settlement at Skara Brae did not survive the storm, yet that very storm which ends the fiction story happened in fact and allowed the homes and their contents to be preserved in sand until it was uncovered by a similarly severe storm in the mid-nineteenth century, revealing the existence, otherwise unrecorded, of a Stone Age settlement of folk who died leaving all their possessions for posterity.

The foreword of Kathleen Filder's absorbing story introduces the readers to the facts of the case. We can imagine the village as it is now, an interesting archaeological find, and as it was in Stone Age times, homes for a settlement of people surviving in a harsh environment. The fiction brings the dwellings alive to the young reader/listener. The authenticity helped to give an understanding of that early period in man's existence which I wished to convey to the young children with whom I worked on this topic.

We are told that as the sand was stripped away seven stone huts connected by passage ways were found with a central paved 'market place' area. Stone furniture was found in the huts: paved floors, stone hearths, stone beds and cupboards, stone seats, water tanks and dressers. Treasures such as stone hammers, axes, knives, carved balls, bowls and necklaces of bones and animal teeth were found. All these artefacts are woven into Mrs Fidler's story in an ingenious fashion.

Since she is an author who understands her child audience, the story surges along with adventures and excitement in each of its short chapters, the scene being set and the description woven into the fabric of the adventure. Young children spin their own pictures as they listen with interest to the happenings of their heroes and heroines. The book's pictures (by Edward Mortelmans) are few but reasonably effective. The book is not well presented by Puffin, but the excellence of the story encouraged many readers in the class to read it for themselves whilst I, as the instigator of these history studies, read the book in sections, prior to discussion and research.

Reference books on Stone Age and Bronze Age societies were called upon for additional and confirming information. Their pictures added to the children's understanding and increased their enthusiasm. A BBC television programme gave us other views of Skara Brae as it exists today. The fictional story made it very clear to the children that life without wood is possible, but difficult. It *was* difficult to imagine life on an island without trees.

*Kali sat up in her stone bed filled with heather and thrust aside the skeepskin robe which covered her.*

The opening sentence begins to set the scene for our heroine's life style. The inside of the little home is described as Kali moves about the one-roomed hut, beginning her morning chores by adding peat fuel to the glowing embers of an all-night fire. A stone slab acts as a door leading into the passage-way beyond. A gap in the wall leads on to the sand dunes and down to the beach in front of the beehive-domed huts. Kali and her brother climb onto the rocks in search of shell fish for food. Birno, their father, is a stone mason. His work is to help shape the stones erected in the building of a temple to their Sun God. Their only tools are made of stone and flint.

The children needed reminding that this story took place more than 1000 years before Jesus was born. Such concepts of time are difficult enough for adults to envisage and virtually impossible for children. I try to help them by suggesting it takes four generations in a family to span 100 years. Therefore, including themselves, their parents, grandparents and great-grandparents, they will have travelled 100 years back in time. The problem is to imagine ten such spans! We have to decided to think of it as a long, long time.

Members of this close community are shown to have had respect for each other and each other's possessions. There was a rough justice and a strong social commitment. They depended on each other by sharing skills: stone masons, potters, fishermen, hunters, sheep farmers. They collected peat for fuel, and heather and bracken for bedding. They were a religious people, with traditions and customs laced with superstitions. Since they were so far north, the summer sun brought them warmth and plenty. It was 'life' to them and they worshipped it. The long dark days of winter brought cold and hardship.

The author studied the archaeological findings and geographical facts of the area. It is obvious in reading the story that she has 'done her homework'. The classroom teachers had confidence in the facts intertwined with the fictional situation. It is good for the children to verify details and practise their reference skills. It brings excitement of a different sort to find confirmation of a story's detail in a more formal text and to see in a picture elsewhere an object met in the tale.

Our story children are in danger and are rescued by a boy, Tenko. He is a stranger from the mainland and brings with him two marvels, a wooden boat and a bronze axe, two materials unknown to the people of Skara Brae. The gleaming bronze tool is a magical thing.

The children in the story compare notes about their different life styles and the listeners in my class learned more about the conditions of these early times. As they identified themselves with the children in the story, so history came alive in their imaginations and concepts which are difficult to teach became accepted. Talk and writing, drawing and drama confirmed their understanding and grasp of the facts. Enthusiasm carried us through our studies, and personal researches in certain areas chosen by the children were undertaken in responsible maturing ways. As their teacher, I did not have to persuade or cajole, but to open the book, read, begin discussion, provide resources, help with further information, find and indicate presentable ways to produce their work.

This class of children will remember the Skara Brae stoy of Kali and Tenko long after they forget the numerous reference books that pleased them in their usefulness. Yet the combined knowledge they had absorbed from listening to the story and corroborating facts will stay with them for many years to come.
*Tales read with pleasure singly or shared are remembered for a lifetime; the contents of a textbook have a less assured survival* (Meek, 1977).

**A.M. Thorne, MA, BEd,**
*Headteacher, Limbrick Wood Junior School*

## Case Study 2

*Beowulf* in the Special School

(A brief account of the presentation of the 'Beowulf' story — based largely on Rosemary Sutcliff's book *Beowulf: Dragon Slayer* — to pupils on the 10-15 age range at Tyntesfield Special School)

It has always seemed to me logical to present tales from the great oral traditions of literature to those children who are failing to read. Had these children been born a few centuries earlier — before our Western society, and certainly our education system, became obsessed with the acquisition of literacy — they would have been quite capable of enjoying these stories, and in my experience they still are. It is often difficult to choose suitable examples of modern children's books to read to slow learners, and for many years the Greek myths, stories of King Arthur and other hero tales have been my starting point.

There are practical advantages in telling stories rather than reading them, particularly to children who are not accustomed to listening to stories, or who may be disruptive. Eye contact can be maintained, and the hands used for restraining or emphasising gestures; the setting of the story, especially with my small groups, can be informal; difficulties of interpretation can be anticipated and incorporated into the story; the children's reactions can be more easily observed; and most important of all, the story can come before the book. To the illiterate child, books themselves can be a barrier to enjoyment, a barrier which can be perpetuated through the generations if the chain is not broken early on by an enlightened approach to story telling.

The main disadvantage in telling rather than reading a story is in the amount of preparation involved. I had not used Beowulf in school until last year, when I began teaching older ESN children for the first time. One class had responded well to my 'introductory' story, Theseus and the Minotaur, and remembering how much my own son had enjoyed *Beowulf: Dragon Slayer*, I re-read Rosemary Sutcliff's novel, and also looked at two more: Ian Serraillier's *Beowulf* and *Beowulf: a new telling* by Robert Nye. I was already familiar with June Oldham's *The Raven Waits* which I had bought after meeting her at a conference, but I thought this rather complex for my audience. My first step was to get to know my material extremely well, so that I could tell the story in every detail, and was able to visualise in my mind's eye all the scenes of the action as if it were a play: the Hall, the coastline, the surrounding countryside, Grendel's lair, and the whole atmosphere of the times. I pronounced them incorrectly, but at least my errors would be consistent! I also made a forecast of the directions in which I thought 'follow-up' work might go, although this is always a dangerous practice with these children; anything can happen, from the project collapsing altogether to the whole idea taking off.

I began by asking the children to imagine they were sitting, not in their small mobile classroom, but in a great hall, with its floor covered in herbs and straw, long trestle tables, and a blazing wood fire. A seaman is telling a story, and in the smoke-filled room, faces glow in the firelight as men bend closer to the story teller, listening intently, their hearts beating in fear. This is not pleasant fairy tale they are hearing...and this is the sailor's story...

My sessions with these children were short — 20 minutes at the end of another lesson if I was lucky — which meant that I had to create the right atmosphere very quickly in order to reach my planned 'suspense points' at which to finish. I also needed to respond to the children's reactions: facial expressions usually indicate shared emotion, amusement, terror and personal involvement, as well as degrees of concentration or boredom. I have to be prepared to change my approach if interest wanes, and perhaps introduce some impromptu acting, or other kinds of audience participation — or to abandon the tale altogether if it is obviously not successful. The reasons for this vary, and I have learned to accept that however well I choose my material, a windy day, a school event, or even one child in a difficult mood, can disrupt everything, and trial and error is the only way to find out whether children enjoy a story. Fortunately there were no problems with Beowulf, and the flow of the story was able to be continued uninterrupted at least until the end of the lesson — although I sometimes changed my 'finishing point' according to the mood of the class. I was surprised how the children accepted the strange names, and even the vocabulary, when after two or three lessons I began reading extracts from the Rosemary Stucliff version. Wyrd appeared to be accepted as a god-like figure, and did not invite comment; I find with the Greek myths that the 'gods' are happily interpreted from a Christian viewpoint. The function of the Wergild was not questioned. The only word which a child queried was Grendel's 'lair' — I had used the word 'hide-out' in my story.

There is seldom much feed-back from slow learners, who appear to accept or enjoy material and then forget it quite quickly; but most of the children remembered the finishing point of the previous lesson, and I allowed a few minutes for 'recap' at the start of the sessions. I overheard one child telling another in the playground about the 'brilliant story' they had heard, and we were regaled one lunchtime with the gory details of Grendel's torn arm. The monster's defeat in Heorot was definitely the high-spot of the story; interest flagged a little in the succeeding account of

Beowulf's battle with Grendel's mother but the death of Beowulf brought outraged cries from some. I did not feel competent to tell that part of the story, and the drama of Rosemary Stucliff's account seemed to be sensed by my listeners; there was much discussion stimulated by the hero's demise.

Several of the children drew or painted pictures of the book, especially of Grendel — but it was obvious that they found it difficult to imagine what he looked like. One boy painted the return of Beowulf, and another attempted a model of the Great Hall. I used the opportunity created by a colleague's absence to show the 'Sutton Hoo' slides to the three classes who had heard the Beowulf story, but these, despite careful selection, only interested a small minority, although they prompted some ideas for pattern making in art. We talked about the whole saga at the end of term, and most of the children seemed to have a good grasp of its structure. One of the girls asked if she could borrow my copy of *Beowulf: Dragon Slayer.* She said she enjoyed reading it, but she is not an articulate child, and although she appears to be a capable reader, it is hard to assess whether this was true.

It was the idea of one of the boys to make a model of Grendel's arm — obviously the most vivid 'picture' in the book — to hang on the art room wall as a talking point — rather like the tiger skin on the wall of the game hunter, and we will be spending some time next term dabbling in plaster, chicken wire and red paint. There will be more 'follow-up' lessons in drama and music, and the children have already begun work on background percussion music for a radio play of the story.

Measures of success are not easy, although I think we would all describe the story of Beowulf as an enjoyable shared experience which has given us new insight into our past, and I feel sure that it will be a long time before the children of Tyntesfield forget *Beowulf: Dragon Slayer.*

**M. Llewellyn**
*Tyntesfield Special School*

## Case Study 3

### *The Children's Crusade*, Henry Treece (Bodley Head, 1971, and Puffin); *Knight Crusader,* Ronald Welch (Oxford, 1954)

This was a topic which I undertook with a class of 34 children, aged 8-9, of mixed ability. The primary aim was to use the two books to give some knowledge of the history of the crusades. I intended that the children would expand this work through their English work, art and craft, religious studies and some geography. *The Children's Crusade, 1212* is well down on the list of crusades and *The Knight*

*Crusader* is set at the time of the third crusade, so before beginning the books I set the scene with some history/geography lessons. The children traced a large outline map of Europe and continued around the Mediterranean and North African coastline, marking in the main countries, the Black Sea and cities of Rome, Jerusalem and Istanbul (Constantinople). From previous work, the children were aware of 'the Roman Empire', and we began a date line at 1 AD. General discussion established the meaning of pilgrimage and the importance of the Holy Places to Christians. The next date was 1000 AD and we put in the first crusade at 1096 AD and mentioned the new centre of civilisation — Constantinople. Halfway came 570 AD the year of Mahomet. The story of Mahomet was given and new vocabulary introduced — Allah, Islam, Moslem, mosque.

To introduce arms and armour, I took chapter three of *Knight Crusader,* filling in the background and reading the section on preparing for battle. I used this for drawing work, the children putting in as much activity and detail into their pictures as possible. Their imaginations were stimulated by the story and a lot of information garnered on the importance of horses and water; exchanging horses; knight's equipment; the feudal system, and the self- sufficiency of castle life.

Now I began to read *The Children's Crusade*. For this age group, I thought the book needed editing, so I began with the postscript, 'About this book'. This introduced Stephen of Cloyes. I gave a synopsis of the beginning of the book and the main characters, Alys, Geoffrey, Brother Gerard and Robert de Villacours. The story, for my purposes, began at chapter seven, where Stephen appears at Beauregard. We had an animated discussion on Stephen's character, and his motives for taking the children on crusade, with prediction work. I moved to chapters nine and ten, the journey with Stephen. The story of the sick five-year old gained the sympathy of the class and led to written work on her story. Why had she left home? Did she return? What did her parents do?

Prediction work again — what would happen to the chalice? I introduced the character of the piper, giving the description from chapter five. A spin-off here to the Pied Piper of Hamelin and art work to paint or make a collage of the piper of the story. To keep a direct story line, I continued to where the children were approaching Marseilles. Chapter 15, 'Duel with the Sea', was the highlight of the book as far as listening was concerned and the children were totally absorbed. Again this produced good art/craft work, with a frieze showing the main story being built up. Drama work came in here too — acting out the story with parts for everyone. I continued through chapters 16 and 17, stopping where Geoffrey and Alys became separated boarding the boats. The children were agog to know what happened to Alys and as there is a good gap in the story before we actually hear, they were kept guessing long enough to write their own stories. The children brought in lots of background details to their stories and wrote very imaginatively projecting themselves into the story. I then completed the book.

The work so far had taken just over half a term and I reviewed it with the class. The girls decided they had enjoyed *The Children's Crusade* but the boys had also enjoyed the battles and fighting of *Knight Crusader*.

For atmosphere of battle, I read to the children the description of the trek across the desert and the battle at Hattin from *Knight Crusader*. It is a straightforward account, easy to read and clear to the children who used it effectively as background material for their own stories. The book was also useful for a comparison of life at home with life in Outremer and led to work on 'Coming home from the Crusades'.

We then produced an assembly based on the children's efforts showing slides of the Holy Land today, telling the story of their work and displaying the pictures they had produced. Prayers were about peace, sharing possessions, for world leaders, tolerance to the view of others, service to others (we had referred to the St John's Ambulance Brigade whilst studying the Knights Templars), and courage in adversity.

Over all this was an enjoyable topic, the stories making the history come alive for the children so that the acquisition of knowledge was a fairly painless process. The children were keen to look for information, discussion was valuable, art opportunities plentiful, and by the end of the term each child had produced a good folder of work.

**M. Hamil**
*St Thomas More School, Coventry*

## Case Study 4

### *The Spaniards are Coming,* Ruth Manning-Sanders (Heinemann); *Fireships Away: the inside story of the Spanish Armada*, Harry T. Sutton (National Trust)

(Work done in two classrooms using historical fiction with ten year olds)

The work described was carried out with two separate classes of ten year-old boys during timetabled history lessons — in the spring term of 1985. The boys are pupils in an independent junior school and have all passed an entrance test to enter the school. Within that framework they are taught as mixed ability classes having a subject based timetable. Each lesson lasts about 40 minutes.

The history curriculum for ten year olds covers the Tudor and Stuart period in English history. They have a double lesson — one hour and 20 minutes each week. I find this an exciting period to teach and generally get a good response from the children. It is quite possible to combine art and history as I teach them both, but I wanted to help the boys feel what it was like to live in Elizabethan times — particularly at the time of the Armada in 1588.

I began to look for some appropriate historical fiction to use in my lessons. I felt this was one of the best ways of involving the children at their level and giving them both enjoyment and information. It was not easy to find any suitable stories that were not too long, for the historical period that I wanted. Most fiction dealing with the Tudors — like *Cue for Treason* by Geoffrey Trease — was too long for the limited time available. I particularly wanted the story to reinforce my teaching and coincide as far as possible. In the end I discovered two short books.

The first was *The Spaniards are Coming* by Ruth Manning-Sanders. This is in the series 'Long Ago Children' especially written to feature 'boys and girls of different periods in an authentic historical setting'. The story tells of a brother and sister who travelled the roads of England with their father in the reign of Queen Elizabeth I. They are acrobats and jugglers, but one day their father is press-ganged into the Queen's service to fight the Spaniards. The children are motherless and they run away from a Justice of the Peace and try to reach their great-uncle in Plymouth. They have a dog who goes with them on their journey.

The second book chosen was *Fireships Away: the inside story of the Spanish Armada* by Harry T. Sutton. It is published in the National Trust series of historical stories connected with National Trust properties and written for children. The story begins 'On Beacon Hill' and tells how the children (again brother and sister) assist their father to get their beacon lit when the Armada is sighted. It also described how they see the Armada becalmed off Sussex. Then the scene changes to aboard one of the commander's ships with the English fleet off Calais and so the 'inside story' of the Armada is told.

I read the stories aloud at the end of each lesson over a period of about six weeks, during which time the Armada was being taught, written about, and painted. The children became absorbed in them and asked questions and made comments at the end of each reading. They were obviously enjoyed because they were good stories in which the children felt able to participate. 'It really made me think as though I was actually there. I really enjoyed it' was written about *The Spaniards are Coming*. Also 'it is a very good book and I would like to read it again myself'. Another comment, about *Fireships Away*, was that 'I could visualise it happening, especially the fire ships being set alight'.

For many of the boys it obviously contributed to their understanding of the period — comparisons were made with the present day when they discussed the stories with me at the end of each chapter. At the beginning of *The Spaniards are Coming* the two children are in the house of the Justice of the Peace, a local Cornish squire. They have been performing their acts in the kitchen in order to earn a meal. Several children commented on the class system in operation as shown by the squire's treatment of the children. Also great surprise was shown at the way the children were left entirely on their own to look after themselves. 'It couldn't happen to me now,' said one boy. Later in the story they were interested in the glimpses of life — the poor house in which the two children are given hospitality, the beggars and other folk met on the road to the town, the cruel punishments administered, the value of money. All these were discussed and remembered. This is what one boy wrote about a month after hearing the story: 'I like the way the story described the town, I imagined that it was full of all sort of people: joyful jugglers and dirty crooks, and also beggars making sores all over their faces. I did not know a town could have such variety.' Another said: 'I learned that people in the Elizabethan times were very kind and they would take in anyone who did not have a home'. One boy was very surprised to learn 'what a tough life children had and they even had to work for their food'. The stirrings of a social conscience are developing here perhaps.

I certainly felt I achieved my aim in trying to broaden the children's understanding of the historical period about which they were learning. One boy's comments seem to sum up the value gained:

*The Spaniards are Coming*: 'I liked this book because it described what England was like in Elizabeth's reign. It added to my knowledge of the Armada and helped us understand what it must have been like for the English at the time. I certainly like it though because an actual boy was telling the story.'

*Fireships Away*: 'I feel just the same about this book except that it is just told ordinarily. I liked the mixture between fact and fiction.'

I would certainly use historical fiction again to help children feel and imagine what it was like to live then. Next time I would go further and discuss more fully the way historical fiction is written, using both facts and imagination. To most children this is not a difficult conception; they frequently combine both elements in their own story writing.

**Penny Birt**
*Warwick Junior School*

## Case Study 5

*Edge,* Merlin Price (Rex Collings, 1981)

This account must begin with a confession. In pursuing my interest in the use of fiction in topic work with junior children I was in the fortunate position of teaching in a school in Fenny Compton, only a few miles away from the site of the Battle of Edge Hill, and also to have just published a children's novel based on the history and folklore surrounding that event. Although my being the author of the book added certain dimensions to the work done by the children, the approaches outlined would be equally suitable to any other piece of historical fiction which has a strong sense of place.

Having read the story to my class we decided to pay a number of visits to the area. The first visit was seen purely as an affective experience. We were careful to avoid the 'death by a thousand worksheets' syndrome, which can so utterly destroy the imaginative response to such a visit. We were fortunate in timing our first visit to take place on the anniversary of the battle. We arrived early in the morning and crept down the hillside, looking across the fields where Radway and Kineton were shrouded in mist — a magical and rather eerie sight. The children spread out and sat on their own, free to soak in the atmosphere and to jot down thoughts or sketches. This preliminary visit was followed up with others that allowed children to complete their writing and re-work their drawings. Returning to such tasks over a number of sessions produced a higher quality of work, and allowed time for this initial experience to be internalised. A hurried sketch and a scribbled poem are all too often the meagre harvest of a single visit.

*I feel the battle a long time ago.*
*It comes towards me.*
*I hear the drums.*
*The Captain waves the flag.*
*The battle starts right now.*
*I hear the cannons from a long way away.*
*The dead people turn to ghosts.*
*Soon the battle will be ended.*
*The people fight in the midnight.*
*The battle ends with fear.*
*The people scream.*

That is an example of a piece of writing done by one of the less-able members of the class as a response to the first visit. Several weeks later the class had an opportunity to examine an antique pistol of the kind used at the battle and featured in my novel. The following poem shows that even though considerable time had elapsed, the initial experience was still very much in mind:

*Feel this gun.*
*It feels so round, so delicate.*

*Yet in battle it is used as a drinking glass is used.*
*It's slopped around.*
*It's killed twenty or thirty people.*
*I am now the murderer in charge of this gun.*
*Yet I have not murdered them.*
*Instead of a glass shattering, it shatters bones.*
*Instead of the glass containing wine it contains the blood of dead victims.*
*The gun is three hundred years old.*
*This gun is a deadly weapon.*
*Gunpowder and a bullet and the gun is happy.*
*Will I hit or miss my target the gun says to itself.*
*The one bullet is fired.*
*A bang and a person is dead.*
*A piece of metal, a dose of gunpowder, can kill a person.*
*How can a piece of metal smaller than a person kill?*

These creative responses to the book and the visits generated interest which facilitated the pursuit of more purely historical objectives. Novels may romanticise or over-simplify events, but textbooks present a pre-digested view which does little to engage the emotions, develop critical thinking or encourage the skill of empathy. *Edge* had involved study of local first-hand sources and among these was an opportunity for investigation small enough to be handled by juniors. There was a record of an incident during the battle when the King's Standard was purloined by Parliamentarians, and regained by fair means or foul, depending on which account you read. The children were provided with copies of several accounts, which showed quite biased viewpoints of the same events. Follow-up discussions and tasks included writing a front-page story of the incident for a newspaper sympathising with either the Royalist or Parliamentarian cause. This was successful across the entire junior age range but care must be taken in seeking out events that involve conflict and controversy. By the end of the activities children were unwilling to accept textbook accounts at face value any more. 'But what was the other side of the story?' they asked.

A final aspect of the work was an examination of continuity and change in the area around Edge Hill. Looking at maps, after going through the sequence of activities outlined above, greatly enhanced their work on basic maps skills. Rather than being presented with some sterile map-reading task, the children were provided with copies of maps of the area from three different periods and spent several hours pouring over them, excitedly recognising places they had visited. Again, you cannot underestimate the importance of allowing sufficient time for this activity. Gradually they began to pinpoint specific differences in the maps and discovered the need to communicate positions to other groups. Thus co-ordinates and bearings came within their ken not as some abstract exercise, but arising from a very real need. Lists of differences were made, and these required further visits to the area in order to confirm various hypotheses. An example of such a problem concerned The Case of the Vicarage Windows. On the oldest map the vicarage had 'bumps' on its frontage which the children correctly interpreted as some form of bay window. The two later maps showed a straight frontage. We revisited the vicarage and to our amazement the bay windows were still intact. The children decided that no change had occurred, but that the newer maps had been drawn by people who had not give such attention to detail. That hypothesis appears to be totally in keeping with the facts. The important point is that the children had been engaged in an exercise that had involved some critical thinking — a long way from colouring in the capitals of the world in 'Maps Can Be Fun', volume 13!

**Merlin Price**
*Headmaster, Henley-in-Arden Junior and Infant School*

## Case Study 6

### *The Children of the House,* by Philippa Pearce and Brian Fairfax-Lucy (Longman, 1968, and Puffin)

In the spring of 1983 I chose to make a classroom study using the book *The Children of the House,* Philippa Pearce's adaptation of the story by Brian Fairfax-Lucy.

As a social document this book represents a curious mixture of childhood memories and reflected social attitudes. What it captures so vividly, however, is the special private world of childhood and the atmosphere of life in a Victorian household on a large country estate. The story, concerning the lives of the Hatton family at the beginning of this century, was one that I was certain my class of third- and fourth-year juniors would enjoy. It seemed particularly suitable as the school was situated only a few miles from Charlecote, home of the Lucy family and the 'house' featured in the book.

As I read aloud the story of the four Hatton children: their secret adventures, conversations with each other, servants and parents, my pupils' growing involvement with the family was expressed by the desire to explore and develop various themes and relationships. The activities and work which both accompanied and followed my readings showed how much the children had identified with the main characters: Laura, Tom, Hugh and Meg. The approach was through drama, the children re-enacting scenes from the story and going on to improvise, write scripts and tape record the further adventures of the Hatton family. Research into background details led eventually to art work which included collage and illustrations using scraperboard and coloured inks.

The story records that life is not easy for the four Hatton children for, whilst living in a great house, their parents, Lord and Lady Hatton, appear remote and uncaring. It is mainly the servants and estate workers who provide the models for adult behaviour as they protect and show affection for the children. It is the 'children's' response to each other, their mutual support, kindness and sense of adventure which encourages empathy. My pupils showed a strong desire to recreate fragments of those lives so different from their own. Ten year-old Eleanor recorded: 'I found that when we were doing our play we had to really go with what the people were doing, what they were like. We had to sort of go in their shoes, so that we knew — we had to stay in character or it would sort of spoil the play.' Restricted initially to two or three exciting episodes and working in small groups my class performed to each other, then discussed and refined their individual roles. A taped discussion early in the study reveals one group's reactions to part of the story:

Eleanor: *I feel sorry for the children — really their father's so hard on them — they just get bread and milk and they're not allowed to enjoy the main things in life really, that go with...um...people. I think the servants were nice to them though.*

Sally: *Yes — especially Elsie — I like her — nice.*
All: *Yes.*
Tanya: *I mean — Sir Robert opening the children's letters.*
All: *Yes.*
Eleanor: *I wouldn't like my father opening letters.*

Curiosity about the 'house', its rooms and grounds grew and, although it was not possible to make a visit at that time, slides, photographs and booklets provided many answers. Gradually the children progressed to creating situations and adventures for the Hatton household. These included: Lord Hatton demanding that the local clergyman should discuss the dismissal of the radical and outspoken schoolmaster, family prayers, an accident involving the new car and servants gossiping over an evening meal.

**Extracts from 'Tea in the Kitchen' by Samantha Wild:**
Scene: At the end of a long working day, all the servants gather in the kitchen, and chat all about the village gossip, and the Hattons. (Enter Walter and Elsie and Ernest)
Walter: *Well, Mrs Ashley, what have we got today.*
Mrs Ashley: *Rabbit stew.*
Elsie: *Oh.*
Ernest: *Well, let's get started.*
Alice: *No, dear Hortense is not here, we cannot start without her.*

Walter: *What's the latest gossip?*
Elsie: *Well [pause] I hear there's been a row between the vicar and the schoolmaster, and the schoolmaster is going to leave.*
Alice: *I heard that the schoolmaster only came because Evie wanted fresh air. Now she's dead, there's nothing to hold him here.*
Ernest: *Walter, what's the latest in cricket, I haven't been able to see the newspaper, as I have been rushed off my feet.*
*Walter: Well, oh here's Hortense* [enter Hortense]
Mrs Ashley: *Here is your rabbit stew, Hortense.*
Hortense: *Rabbit stew.*
Mrs Ashley: *Yes. Did you know, Alice, that the price of milk has gone up again, oh and while I come to think of it, Dan hasn't been getting enough rabbits and partridges. Alice will you go down to Dan, tomorrow, and ask him for some more.*
Alice: *Yes Mrs Ashley.*
Elsie: *That Miss Laura, she's a proper big lass, she is getting grown up now, too.*
Walter: *Aye. Master Hugh, he's getting clever now, I'd say he's cleverer than Master Tom.*
Ernest: *Did you know that there might be war against Germany.*
Elsie: *No [worriedly] oh I hope not.*
Mrs Ashley: *I doubt it. Are you all enjoying your stew? It's a new recipe.*
Hortense: *Lady Hatton is going to a dinner party tonight.*
Elsie: *What dress is Lady Hatton wearing?*
Hortense: *Lady Hatton is wearing her silk dress.*
Elsie: *Ooooh, Lady Hatton is lucky.*
Hortense: *Yes. [Far away a bell rings] Oh, there goes the bell for Lady Hatton's room. I must go, goodbye.*

As interest grew, so did the demand for further information. The illustrations to the book proved difficult to interpret when planning art work and this prompted the children to seek out various details from reference books and photographs. In this way they were able to record accurately the children's clothes, servants' uniforms and suitable evening wear for Lord and Lady Hatton. A collection of appropriate material was made, cotton prints, lace and velvet, and portraits of individuals and groups were designed.

The final chapters of the book took the class by surprise when, like Meg in the story, gripped by the dramatic events leading to the outbreak of the First World War, they found it hard to come to terms with sudden and dramatic changes. As Tom and Hugh go off to fight and Laura eventually leaves home to become a nurse, only Meg remains 'a child'. In class, discussions were initiated on the subject of war, women's role in society and social change and many children followed up their keen interest in the period by reading *A Question of Courage* by Marjorie Darke, and Joan Clarke's *Early Rising*. For the older children in the class, already developing an ability to analyse, the search for fact, detail and accuracy was emerging:

Samantha: *I don't think their father was as hard as they made him out to be.*

All: *No — no.*

Sally: *He looked, when we saw the picture [slide] — he looked quite young.*

All: *And handsome — yes.*

Samantha: *And I expected him to be old, harsh.*

Sally: *Yes in my mind I pictured him as a great, big, burly fellow.*

All: *Yes.*

Eleanor: *Well you pictured him wrong!*

Many questions remained unanswered but the gap between fact and fiction was of secondary importance. For my pupils the 'children of the house' were very real, and continued to gather substance through discussion, drama and art.

This approach to the study of social history was, from a professional point of view, immensely enjoyable and highly productive. The story 'written from a memory of a way of life now vanished' (Fairfax-Lucy, author's note), proved a powerful force in generating enthusiastic response. By way of a postscript I would like to add that later in the year my class visited Charlecote, where, dressed as members of the Lucy family and servants, together with members of the National Trust Theatre in Education Group, they re-enacted a story based on the events of earlier Victorian times. For my pupils it was a magical experience — it was, after all, 'their house'!

**Irene Proudman**
*Bishop's Tachbrook School, Warwickshire*

# •*History in Depth through Historical Fiction?*

*But history, real solemn history, I cannot be interested in. Can you?* Jane Austen

We have seen in the previous section the work which children's historical fiction can inspire in schools. We would now like to study the propositions of the first section in more detail and give some particular examples of the ways in which good historical fiction can enable a study of history in depth which is quite impossible from the general run of textbooks.

We would like to consider the best historical fiction for children in one particular era, that of the Anglo-Saxons. It came as a surprise to an in-service group of students how long a period of our national history Anglo-Saxon England was and how important it had been to our cultural development. The achievements of Anglo-Saxon civilisation in the tenth and eleventh centuries have recently been emphasized by an exhibition at the British Museum. Permanently on display there are the grave goods of the Sutton Hoo ship burial, whose beauty and mystery many textbooks for children have attempted to utilize, and the Lindisfarne Gospels which surely must rank among the great works of art of all time. Between the age of Bede and the Lindisfarne Gospels and the age of St Dunstan and the Benedictional of St Æthelwold Anglo-Saxon England underwent a test of fire — the raids and invasions of the Vikings. It survived and ultimately, under the leadership of the kings of Wessex, all England was united and the foundations were laid for another cultural golden age. It so happens that what we consider to be one of the best novels for children deals with the moment when Anglo-Saxon resistance to Viking expansion begins to take root: C. Walter Hodges' *The Namesake* (1964). It is just how deeply this work takes children into the past that we wish to demonstrate.

*The Namesake* reveals to the young reader a whole world of long ago, yet at the same time it is a study of Anglo-Saxon kingship at a moment of crisis in its development. We see the kings divided among themselves: the hatred of Mercia for Wessex is stronger than the fear of the Danes (p. 39 — all page references are to the Puffin edition, 1967). Edmund of East Anglia and Ethelred and Alfred of Wessex are very conscious that they are defending a Christian society against paganism (pp. 15, 16, 105) but only Alfred gets right the balance between piety and self-reliance. We see the king taking counsel with bishops and ealdormen through whom he rules the shires of his kingdom (pp. 115, 119). The ealdormen are the leaders of the local forces and the rank and file can feel more loyal to them than to their king (pp. 55, 56). Alfred has the charismatic personality to overcome this localism, but he combines this with an awareness of the importance of organization: hence his regulation of the fyrd and the creation of the embryonic navy, his building of a capital city and his realization of the importance of literacy to efficient government (pp. 127, 141, 153, 155, 156, 172).

This is all set firmly in its material background. To survive in that age a king or nobleman has always to be accompanied by his bodyguard of warriors. The social life, both of the king's hall and on a royal manor, is shown (pp. 89, 120). We are made conscious that it is the peasantry which forms the vast majority of the population. Over the peasants the fighting passes and they are its chief victims. The ceorls, their villages, their limited horizons and loyalties and the tension between resisting the invader and farming the land are all portrayed (pp.20, 21, 101, 102). The fact that Anglo-Saxon society was slave owning and less egalitarian than its enemies' is not ignored, and Hodges' view is that the bondmen were descendants of the original inhabitants of Britain and that they were indifferent to the national struggle (pp. 33, 78-80). Throughout we are reminded of the low level of material existence for the majority. At night wolves howl in the omnipresent forest (p.102).

The Anglo-Saxon church is shown to be well past its first golden age. Its achievements in literacy, art and building (stone building is now a rarity) are in decline, and the faithful, especially when recently converted, hold a strange mixture of Christian and pagan beliefs (pp. 8, 9, 10, 11, 62). Yet Christianity is still capable of generating fanaticism as exemplified by the terrifying but ultimately pathetic figure of Esdras.

Above all it is the convincing image of the Danish raiders, in the textbooks either monsters or supermen, which is one of the outstanding achievements of the novel. Danish kings are merely leaders of war bands and there is intense rivalry between them (p. 166). Guthorm (Guthrum) is a totally intelligible figure. Of humble origin he is driven by consuming ambition to achieve fame and is possessed of the necessary cunning and physical prowess:

*This Guthorm was of middle height, with coarse red hair which he let grow to his shoulders, and a red beard which he clipped short. He had small eyes and bushy eyebrows. He was very strong in body. It was said that he came from Limfjord in Jutland, the younger son of a large family who, having no patrimony, had gone viking in a ship's crew. It was also said that being both cunning and brave he soon came to be the foremost in that crew, and then had diced with the shipman for his ship while the man was drunk, and won it from him, and had slain him afterwards in the quarrel over it. He had brought his own ship and his own crew when he came to England to further his fortunes in Halfdan's army* (p. 122).

*Jarl Guthorm was now in his thirtieth year, and he knew the time was ripe for him, if he were ever to win great fame. He knew his strength and ambition. Now that Halfdan had gone north, and, as Guthorm knew, was not likely to turn again towards Mercia, let alone to Wessex, the Danish army in Mercia was without a king. The chieftains in their Council formed alliances among themselves, all for different reasons, having no great cause or single mind. Guthrom knew that if anyone could unite them in a single cause and hold them in it, he might make and rule a kingdom. This he was resolved to do himself* (p. 138).

But the intelligence and honesty of Alfred baffle him, and he can only attribute his defeat to ill-luck (p. 218).

Hodges accurately portrays the Danish method of raiding, their tactics in battle, the reinforcement of their armies by fresh recruits from overseas (pp. 45, 112, 143). Yet we are reminded that they too were basically peasant farmers whose instinct to plough in spring was as strong as their urge to fight (p. 122). He also gives us an insight into their minds, and they are believable human beings, with virtues and failings like their Anglo-Saxon enemies. They are greedy, cruel and vain, but also brave, with some idea of honour, not without a sense of humour, kind, even sentimental. The scene where a raiding party intercepts a group of Anglo-Saxon refugees is a fine piece of imaginative historical writing:

*'Horses! Horses!,' a voice shouted suddenly in alarm. 'Look over there!' In confusion, wondering what this could be, I looked where the man was pointing, back to the dyke which we had left but could still be seen as a ridge on the horizon. Between it and ourselves a dark line of moving shapes was approaching us over the fields. They were men on horseback, coming at a steady trot and spreading out to head us off and close in on us with our backs to the marshy river which was too wide to cross.*

*'The heathen! Holy Mother protect us, they are the heathen!' cried a woman next to me. Her child, a little girl, clung close against her. 'Holy Mother protect us!' murmured the woman, sinking to her knees and making the sign of the cross.*

*For a moment one or two of our men looked as though they were prepared to make a fight of it, others as if they would try to escape on the two or three horses we had; but a moment's judgment soon showed there was no hope in either course. The oncoming Danes must have numbered more than thirty, all well-armed and mounted, and their wide semicircle, now completely around us, was moving in at a walking pace. Man for man they seemed bigger than the English. They were fair-haired and red-faced. I notice that some of them had bracelets and other pieces of jewellery, and some had embroidered cloaks, but for the most part there was no great show of luxury about them, such as I had expected. Indeed, they had a rather plain, working-day appearance as they trotted up laughing and talking among themselves. We all stood hemmed in and waiting, doing nothing. Two or three of the heathen rode forward and began to drive away our cattle without a word to us. We offered no resistance. The leader of the Danes, a huge man wearing a coat all sewn with iron plates, laughed and called out:*

*'Hola, dog English! Ye be cattle-thieves, hey? Dost though go to slink off sideling, hey? Dost though go creeping? Thou shalt creep on all fours now, shalt thou not? Hoi! Dog English cattle-thieves, what else hast thou stolen, ye dirty jackdaw men? What else have ye hid among your lice hey? Strip, strip, off clothes, off.'*

*The women they drove off to one side with the cattle, and the rest of us were made to strip. The heathen took anything of the least value they could find in our clothes, while we stood shivering naked in the bitter wind...*

*'Swim, swim, all swim!' they cried, and on the spur of the moment with spears and kicks and much laughing they began to drive us all into the river.*

*'Swim, all swim!' they shouted as the last one splashed among the reeds. The victims stood up to their necks, blue with cold and pricked back at the spear's point whenever they tried to clamber out. Only the women and children and myself did they exempt from this game. 'Not thee, thou little one-leg, not thee,' said one of them to me, and he smiled and patted me on the back.*

*A short while after, their leader, who had been away looking over the cattle, rode up, and after joining in the laughter at this sport, presently put two fingers in his mouth and gave a loud whistle.*

*'To horse now, my vikings!' he ordered. 'Away, hoi! Hoi, away!'*

*With hardly a look back at their victims who were at least free to clamber and haul each other out of the water into the November wind, the pagans got on their horses and began to ride off, driving the cattle at a casual pace, talking and laughing among themselves, just as they had come* (pp. 35-38).

'That is just how it must have been' one feels. The brutality is not premeditated, nor indeed intended to be fatal: it is impromptu, casual almost, and mixed in with hard-headed materialism and humanity towards the maimed Alfred Dane-leg.

The overall effect of the novel is to give a haunting picture of the destruction wrought by the Danish armies and to capture the epic quality of the struggle of Wessex for survival. Yet all this is the basic fabric into which is woven the story of the two Alfreds. Both are physically weak, but both face up to life and the responsibilities it thrusts upon them — and both play their parts to the best of their ability.

Hodges' book was first published in 1964 and Anglo-Saxon studies have moved on since then. Teachers can judge how well his scholarship has stood up by testing it against recent studies of Alfred and the Vikings; for example the introduction to S. Keynes and M. Lapidge, *Alfred the Great — Asser's Life of Alfred and Other Contemporary Sources* (1983) and P.H. Sawyer, *Kings and Vikings* (1982). Generally Hodges' history is sound: only in the relationship of Wessex and Mercia does he seem to have been quite wrong, co-operation rather than rivalry being the determining factor. Otherwise the younger readers will not get a misleading picture of the era from this author.

What they will get, because of the story and the detail which the author supplies, is a Tardis-like transportation into the past. When the past becomes as real as this there is a basis for discussion as meaningful and deep as the discussion of the characters and situations in any novel, except that some of the characters actually existed and most of the events actually happened. They will be able to talk about Alfred as a real person and his problems as real situations, something which is not stimulated by the generality of textbooks. History can be as exciting as fiction. But for young readers especially the 'solemnity' of history can be a barrier. Fiction can be a means of overcoming this, but the fiction must be kept under control by the disciplined imagination of the author. Hodges has this quality in *The Namesake*, and the discipline of his writing stems from his knowledge of and empathy with that particular past era.

Inevitably the questions will arise: how does Hodges know all this? what is actual, what is the author's invention in the story? So the pupils are led back to the original sources of the period, to the Anglo-Saxon Chronicle and to Asser's Life of Alfred, now both readily available in modern translations. Here is a quotation from the Anglo-Saxon Chronicle for the year 876 (Garmonsway edition):

*In this year the enemy army slipped past the army of the West Saxons into Wareham; and then the king made peace with the enemy and they gave him hostages who were the most important men next to their king in the army, and swore oaths to him on the holy ring — a thing which they would not do before for any nation — that they would speedily leave his kingdom. And then under cover of that, they — the mounted army — stole by night away from the English army to Exeter. And that year Halfdene*

*shared out the land of the Northumbrians and they proceeded to plough and to support themselves.*
This was one of the sources for Asser's Life written in 893 (Keynes and Lapidge, 1983, pp. 82-83). Together they form the basis for chapters 15-18 of *The Namesake* and show how Hodges' disciplined imagination has fleshed out the original sources, and made them more understandable and exciting to the young student of history.

If one has confidence in the general accuracy of the historical novel, then it can be used as a source itself and subjected to analysis. An attempt has been made above to analyse *The Namesake* and to show how it reveals the Anglo-Saxon world at the end of the ninth century. Children could be asked to extract information as to how a king ruled his country, what the life of the common people — the peasants — was like, how the religion of the Anglo-Saxons differed in belief and practice from that of the Danes, what the strategy and tactics of Danish armies were, how Alfred tried to combat them, etc. Then these should be compared with original sources and information from textbooks (as some of the teachers did in their projects) to check on their accuracy. No author, however good, is incapable of errors, anachronisms and distortions. Indeed spotting these might give a child that 'taste for blood' which Helen Cam said was the origin of her inspiration to be an academic historian. We might add that the only anachronism we have noticed in *The Namesake* is the naming of a reef of rocks as Peveril Point; it could not have been so called in the ninth century.

The skills approach to history then is perfectly compatible with the use of historical fiction, and puts the attempts at deduction and judgment and the critical consideration of evidence in the warmer, emotional context of a story. The analysis applied to *The Namesake* can be applied to any good work of historical fiction, though of course it will be more or less detailed depending on the skill of the author and the age of the intended audience.

*The Namesake* has a sequel, *The Marsh King*, dealing with the second phase of King Alfred's struggle with Guthrum, which is only one degree less satisfying than its predecessor. The story has a sustained tension, which makes it one of the most exicting historical novels for young readers known to us. The Anglo-Saxon period has inspired other fine historical fiction for children. There is Rosemary Sutcliff's *Beowulf: Dragon Slayer*, her retelling of Beowulf, which captures a great deal of the heroic quality of the original, and from which information and ideas concerning early Anglo-Saxon kingship, the attitudes of the warrior elite, the prevalence of the feud, the status of women and the holding of pagan beliefs can be extracted. Kevin Crossley-Holland has produced a version of Beowulf, illustrated by Charles Keeping, and appropriately designed to be read aloud. Unlike the illustrations in Hodges' books, which he drew himself, Keeping's drawings are inadequate. They are too fanciful, too little conditioned by the archaeological evidence. This is particularly galling when there is such a magnificent source as the finds within the Sutton Hoo ship burial. Jill Paton Walsh's *Hengest's Tale* reconstructs the barbarian society of northern Europe before the Anglo-Saxon invasions began in the fifth century and tells the story of the events leading to the tragedy of the fight at Finnsburgh and its aftermath. Crossley-Holland has written three related stories capturing the atmosphere of the conversion of the Anglo-Saxons to Christianity in *Sea Stranger, Fire Brother* and *Earth Father*, and with Jill Paton Walsh he has also produced *Wordhoard*, a superb series of stories spanning Anglo-Saxon history from the early settlement to the Battle of Hastings. The first one in the collection, *The Woodwose,* brilliantly destroys the myth of Anglo-Saxon racial purity. Geoffrey Trease has written his version of the defeat of Guthrum in *Mist over Athelney*. It was published in 1958, nearly ten years befroe *The Marsh King*, and the two treatments are a fascinating contrast in techniques. Henry Treece has retold the story of Hereward the Wake and the final Anglo-Saxon resistance to the Normans in *Man with a Sword.*

The above list is by no means exhaustive. It shows, however, how historical fiction can cover practically the whole of the Anglo-Saxon period, and many of its most important aspects. Also the demands of the novels and stories in reading ability vary greatly. *Beowulf: Dragon Slayer* can grip quite young children by the sheer force of its story, and also older children with learning difficulties as Mrs Llewellyn has shown. *Hengest's Tale* would need good reading ability, and tough-minded children too, though most seem to be so these days. The books cover that wide range of ability found in so many primary and middle school classes and in mixed ability groups in the lower secondary school. Undoubtedly, however, they provide children with a greater opportunity for insight into the Anglo-Saxon period than most textbooks.

Such an assemblage of novels might be produced for almost any period. Perhaps as the more recent past is approached, as the sources grow richer, more personal and easier for children to read themselves, the need for the use of historical fiction is less, and novels should not be so central to the teaching, though this is debatable. Most of the twentieth century is almost as much 'a foreign country' (L.P. Hartley's term for the past) to children in schools today as the Anglo-Saxon era. A number of novels could reinforce lessons on the Second World War by showing how children on the home front experienced the war, particularly bombing and evacuation. One thinks of Robert Westall's *The Machine Gunners,* Susan Cooper's *Dawn of Fear,* Hester Burton's

*In Spite of all Terror*, Nina Bawden's *Carrie's War,* and Michelle Magorian's *Goodnight Mister Tom.* In at least two of these one suspects that the novel is partly an exorcism of the author's own wartime experiences, and they gain in impact because of this. Also Magorian particularly recreates a way of life at the beginning of the war which later twentieth-century economic, social and technological changes have completely destroyed. From these novels the children get an imaginative experience not to be found in most textbooks, and this provides the motivation which leads on to a more serious contemplation and understanding of history.

Finally, some historical novelists raise issues in history which most writers of textbooks seem to avoid or ignore. This may be because textbook writers believe that 'the facts speak for themselves', or they do not wish to prejudice their young readership, or their publishers are fearful of offending some teachers and parents and therefore of losing potential markets. Geoffrey Trease, while stressing the special responsibility of the author who writes for children that his novel should not be a covert political or religious tract, nevertheless is not afraid to explore the theme of racial and religious prejudice in *The Red Towers of Granada.* A brief summary of the plot and a quotation will illustrate the point.

A Nottinghamshire youth, Robin, is expelled from his village because he is believed to have leprosy. This is diagnosed by his parish priest who resents Robin's superior knowledge (Robin is a student, home on vacation from Oxford). Robin, an outcast from his society, meets another outcast: he saves a Jew, Solomon of Stamford, who was being assaulted by footpads in Sherwood Forest. The Jew is a doctor: he recognises Robin's leprosy as a mere skin infection which he can treat. He takes Robin to Nottingham and Robin stays with him in the Jewish ghetto while receiving treatment. He begins to be interested in the doctor's daughter, Susanna, and arouses the suspicion of her fiery brother, David. The years is 1290. Edward I arrives in Nottingham and announces that the Jews are to be expelled from England. His queen, Eleanor, is ill and she secretly sends for Soloman and asks him to obtain the Golden Essence for her from Spain. Solomon agrees, hoping that this service might help to lessen the persecution of his people. Robin, now cured, attempts to return to his village, only to be driven away when it is learned that a Jew has cured him. He therefore accompanies Solomon to Spain in search of the Muslim doctor who can make the Golden Essence. Jewish and Muslim families in Bordeaux, Toledo and Cordova help them in their quest, but they are pursued by a villainous Dominican friar who believes that they are seeking the elixir of life.

The implications of the plot are clear, but Trease shows how prejudice is broken down in the mind of his hero and how common humanity triumphs:

*Moor, Jew, Christian... What difference did it make? 'He is a man,' said Solomon, 'a good man, a man of science and learning. Is his life nothing in the eyes of God?'*

*Months ago, in the Nottingham ghetto, I had come to accept Soloman and his family as true friends, to understand their different ways and to discover that in many other respects there were no differences to divide us. Should I now find it the same with the Moors — people I had grown up to think of as far-off outlandish infidels, kin to the Saracens whome King Edward had warred with on his crusade? Certainly the Spaniards often spoke of them with admiration, and I had an idea that Benjamin and most other Toledo Jews privately considered the Moors more civilised than the Christians* (pp. 123, 124, Puffin edition).

*Riding hard south to Granada, three young men, a Muslim, a Jew, and a Christian all pray together in their different ways (p. 152).*

We know of hardly any textbook which explicitly raises these issues when treating, for examples, the Crusading era. Yet if history is to have relevance, the apparently eternal human problems which it raises ought to be discussed. Geoffrey Trease is not the only children's novelist to deal with these questions. Henry Treece, though much less powerfully, does so in *The Children's Crusade,* and they are the themes of Peter Carter's novels, *Children of the Book* (the siege of Vienna in 1683), *The Sentinels* (the British navy attempting to stop the slave trade in the early nineteenth century), and *Under Goliath* (the beginning of 'The Troubles' in Belfast in 1969). Some older novels, for example Ronald Welch's *Knight Crusader*, though Mrs Hamil shows they may have their uses, almost reinforce racial and religious prejudice, and children should be encouraged to look at them critically. But there is an important role here for the historical novel in overriding from time to time the 'neutrality' of the textbook.

We hope that our examination of principle and exploration of practice have persuaded teachers that historical fiction is a valuable resource for the classroom. For it is our belief and intention that through it, and the capacity of literature to delight, children may acquire an abiding interest in history, real solemn history.

# •*Bibliography*

## (a) Bibliography of historical novels mentioned in the text


| | |
|---|---|
| **Bawden, N.,** | *Carrie's War* (Gollancz, 1973, also Puffin) |
| **Burton, H.,** | *In Spite of All Terror* (Oxford University Press, 1968) |
| **Carter, P.,** | *Children of the Book* (Oxford University Press, 1982)<br>*The Sentinels* (Oxford University Press, 1980)<br>*Under Goliath* (Oxford University Press, 1977, also Puffin) |
| **Clarke, J.,** | *Early Rising* (Cape, 1974) |
| **Cooper, S.,** | *Dawn of Fear* (Chatto and Windus, 1970, also Puffin) |
| **Crossley-Holland, K.,** | *Sea Stranger; Fire Brother; Earth Father* (Piccolo, 1979)<br>*Beowulf* with Charles Keeping (Oxford University Press, 1982)<br>*Wordhoard* with Jill Paton Walsh (Macmillan, 1969, also Puffin) |
| **Darke, M.,** | *A Question of Courage* (Kestrel, 1975) |
| **Fidler, K.,** | *The Boy with the Bronze Axe* (Oliver and Boyd, 1968, also Puffin) |
| **Garfield, L.,** | *Smith* (Constable, 1967, also Puffin) |
| **Harnett, C.,** | *The Load of Unicorn* (Methuen, 1959, also Puffin) |
| **Hodges, C.W.,** | *The Namesake* (Bell, 1964, also Puffin)<br>*The Marsh King* (Bell, 1967, also Puffin) |
| **Magorian, M.,** | *Goodnight Mister Tom* (Kestrel, 1981, also Puffin) |

**Manning-Sanders, R.,** *The Spaniards are Coming* ('Long Ago Children' series, Heinemann, 1969)

**Marryat, Captain,** *Children of the New Forest* (Dent, 1955)

**Nye, R.,** *Beowulf: a new telling* (Hamish Hamilton, 1983)

**Oldham, J.,** *The Raven Waits* (Aguila Publishing, 1982)

**Paton Walsh, J.,** *Fireweed* (Macmillan, 1969, also Puffin)
*Hengest's Tale* (Macmillan, 1969, also Puffin)

**Pearce, P., Fairfax-Lucy, B.,** *The Children of the House* (Longman, 1968, also Puffin)

**Peyton, K.M.,** *Flambards* (Oxford University Press, 1967)
*The Edge of the Cloud* (Oxford University Press, 1969, also Puffin)

**Power, E. and R.,** *Boys and Girls of History* (Oxford University Press, 1953)

**Price, M.,** *Edge* (Rex Collings, 1981)

**Serrailler, I.,** *The Windmill Book of Ballads: Beowulf the Warrior and other poems* (Heinemann, 1962)

**Sutcliff, R.,** *Simon* (Oxford University Press, 1953)
*The Lantern Bearers* (Oxford University Press, 1959)
*Beowulf: Dragon Slayer* (Bodley Head, 1961)

**Sutton, H.T.,** *Fireships Away: the inside story of the Spanish Armada* ('National Trust Series for Children', Heritage Books, 1977)

**Trease, G.,** *Bows against the Barons* (Martin Lawrence, 1934)
*Trumpets in the West* (Blackwell, 1947)
*Mist over Athelney* (Macmillan, 1958)
*Thunder of Valmy* (Macmillan, 1960)
*Hills of Varna* (Macmillan, 1964)
*The Red Towers of Granada* (Macmillan, 1966, also Puffin)

**Treece, H.,** *Man with a Sword* (Oxford University Press, 1962, also Puffin)
*The Children's Crusade* (Bodley Head, 1958, also Puffin)
*Vinland the Good* (Bodley Head, 1967)

**Welch, R.,** *Knight Crusader* (Oxford University Press, 1954, Oxford Paperback, 1970, New Oxford Library, 1979, also Puffin)

**Westall, R.,** *The Machine Gunners* (Macmillan, 1975, also Puffin)

## (b) Bibliographical resources for historical fiction

Teachers are advised to use their professional judgment rather than publishers' and editors' indications of age ranges.

*Children's Literature: a guide to reference sources*
Library of Congress, 1966

*Historical Novels for Use in Schools*
School Library Association in Scotland, 1970

*Fiction and Non-Fiction Books for Use by the Least Able Pupils in Secondary Schools*
School Library Association in Scotland, 1971

*Fiction, Verse and Legend for Middle and Secondary Schools*
School Library Association, 1978

*Storylines* (series includes historical fiction from pre-history to the present)
Library Association, 1970s.

*Junior Fiction Index* (fourth edition)
London Association of Assistant Librarians, 1981

**Charleton, K.,** *Recent Historical Fiction for Secondary School Children* (Historical Association, TH18, 1960, revised 1969)

**Clark, B.,** *Children's Stories* (School Library Association, 1970)

**Crouch, M.,** *Chosen for Children* (Library Association, 1967), Carnegie Medal Winners 1936-65

**Ellis, A.,** *How to Find Out About Children's Literature* (Pergamon, 1968)

**Eyre, T.,** *British Children's Books in the Twentieth Century* (Longman, 1971)

**Jones, A., Buttray, J.,** *Children and Stories* (Blackwell, 1970)

## (c) Journals concerned with children's literature

Many articles about and by authors referred to in the text and bibliographies may be found in the following journals.

*Book Mark*
English Department, Moray House College, Edinburgh, see especially nos. 4, 10, 11, devoted to historical novels.

*Books for Keeps*
School Bookshop Association, see especially nos. 2, 21, 22, 23.

*Books for Your Children*
Books for your Children, Ashbourne, Derbyshire, see especially Vol. 7, no. 4; Vol. 9, no. 3; Vol. 10, no. 4; Vol. 11, no. 3; Vol. 13, no. 4; Vol. 14, no. 1; Vol. 17, no. 2.

*Children's Book Bulletin*
Children's Rights Workshop, London SW8 1BH, see especially no. 3, spring 1980.

*Children's Books for the Year*
Hamish Hamilton and the National Book League

*Children's Literature Abstracts*
International Federation of Library Associations

*Children's Literature in Education*
Agathan Press, New York, see especially nos. 1, 7, 8, 9, 10.

*Dragons Teeth*
National Committee on Racism in Children's Books

*Growing Point*
Margery Fisher

*Horn Book Magazine*
Horn Books

*Junior Bookshelf*
Marsh Hall, Huddersfield

*Junior Education*
Scholastic Publications Ltd.

*The School Librarian*
Journal of School Library Association

*Signal*
Thimble Press

*Signal Review of Children's Books*
Thimble Press

## (d) Select book list


| | |
|---|---|
| **Cam, H.,** | *Historical Novels* (Historical Association, G48, 1961, reprint 1968, 1974) |
| **Firth, C.,** | *Historical Novels* (Historical Association, 51, December 1924) |
| **Fisher, M.,** | *Intent Upon Reading* (Brockham Press, 1964) |
| **Grugeon, E., Walden, P.,** | *Literature and Learning* (Open University, 1978) |
| **Inglis, F.,** | *Promise of Happiness* (Cambridge, 1981) |
| **Meek, M.,** | *Geoffrey Trease* (Bodley Head, 1960)<br>*Rosemary Sutcliff* (Bodley Head, 1962) |
| **Meek, Warlow, Barton,** | *The Cool Web* (Bodley Head, 1977) |
| **Townsend, J.R.,** | *Written for Children* (Garnett Miller, 1965, also Pelican) |
| **Trease, G.,** | *Tales Out of School* (Heinemann, 1964) |
| **Warner, O.,** | *Captain Marryat: a resdiscovery* (Constable, 1963) |

# • *References Cited in the Text*


**Aries, P.,** *Centuries of Childhood* (Penguin Education, 1962)

**Atkinson, D.J., Evans, D.W.,** *New Writers, Young Readers* (Warwick University, Institute of Education, 1977)

**Bradbury, J.,** 'Historical Novels in the Classroom', *Teaching History,* no. 7, Historical Association, 1972

**Burton, H.,** 'The Author as Historical Novelist: one of the elite', in Meek, Warlow, Barton, *The Cool Web* (Bodley Head, 1977)

**Burston, Green,** **(eds),** *Handbook for History Teachers* (Methuen, 1972)

**Cam, H.,** *Historical Novels* (Historical Association, G48, 1961, reprint 1968, 1974)

**Chancellor, V.,** *Medieval and Tudor Britain* (Penguin, 1967)

**Charlton, K.,** *Recent Historical Fiction for Secondary School Children* (Historical Association, TH18, 1960, revised 1969)

**Davies, P.,** *Growing Up in the Middle Ages* (Wayland Press, 1972)

**Davin, A.,** 'History Made Personal', *Times Educational Supplement, 27 August 1967*

**Dickinson A., Lee, P.,** *History Teaching and Historical Understanding* (Heinemann, 1978)

**Edwards, T.,** 'Stories Not History: the historical novels of Cynthia Harnett', *Children's Literature in Education,* no. 9, Ward Lock, 1972.

**Fisher, M.,** *Intent Upon Reading* (Brockhampton, 1961)

**Garvey, B., Krug, M.,** *Models of History Teaching in the Secondary School* (Oxford University Press, 1977)

**Gunning, D.,** *The Teaching of History* (Croom Helm, 1978)

**Hannam, C.,** *A Boy in Your Situation* (Deutsch, 1977)

**HMSO,** *Teaching History* (Ministry of Education Pamphlet, no. 23, 1952)

**Keynes, S., Lapidge M.,** *Alfred the Great: Asser's Life of Alfred and other contemporary sources* (Penguin Classics, 1983)

**Lamont, W.,** *The Realities of Teaching History* (Chatto and Windus, 1972)

**Leeson, R.,** 'The Spirit of What Age?', *Children's Literature in Education,* no. 23, 1976

**Lewis, E.M.,** *Teaching History in Secondary Schools* (Evans, 1960)

**Low-Beer, A.,** 'Books and the Teaching of History in School', *History,* Vol. 59, no. 197, Historical Association, 1974

**Marriott, S., Kenny, M.,** 'Voluntary Fiction Reading', *Education 3-13*, Vol. 12, no. 2, 1984

**Meek, M.,** 'What is a Horse?', *School Librarian,* Vol. 25, no. 1, 1977

**Nash, E.N., Newth, A.M.,** *Britain in the Modern World: the twentieth century* (Penguin, 1967)

**Power, E., Power, R.,** *Boys and Girls of History* (Oxford University Press, 1953)

**Richter, H.,** *Friedrich* (Longman, 1971)

**Schlager, N.,** 'Predicting Children's Choices in Literature: a developmental approach', *Children's Literature in Education,* no. 3, 1978

**Steele, I.,** *Developments in History Teaching* (Open Books, 1976)

**Sutcliff, R.,** 'The Lantern Bearers', in M. Crouch (ed), *Chosen for Children* (Library Association, 1967)

'History is People', in V. Havilland, *Children and Literature* (Bodley Head, 1973)

**Trease, G.,** 'Historical Novelist at Work', *Children's Literature in Education*, Ward Lock, 1972

'Old Writers and Young Readers', in Meek, Warlow, Barton, *The Cool Web* (Bodley Head, 1977)

**Trevor-Roper, H.,** 'Historical Imagination', *The Listener,* 27 February, 1958

**Warnock, M.,** *Imagination* (Fraser and Fraser, 1976)

**Watts, D.G.,** *The Learning of History* (Routledge and Kegan Paul, 1972)

**Welch, R.,** 'Knight Crusader', in M. Crouch (ed), *Chosen for Children* (Library Association, 1967)

**Wood, A.,** 'Historical Novels: the hardest things to sell? A new look at the work of Geoffrey Trease', *Books for Your Children,* Vol. 7, no. 2, 1982.